Acknowledgements are

First, I want to thank my daughter. It was after having her that I felt the need for a story like this to be written. After writing it, she was very supportive. She was my cheerleader, my audience, and my sounding board. It never would have gotten written without the support of my beautiful daughter, Mimi Potter.

When I first started thinking about writing this story, I didn't know where to start. A good friend of mine helped me start. She helped me understand my writing style and the need to use my style, not someone else's. She helped me understand my creativity and how to let it lead me when writing. Thank you, Debi Brimacombe. Your guidance gave me the courage to write this story.

After writing this story, I let it sit on a shelf. Once in a while I would get it out, read it, and get excited about it. But, I was afraid to share it with anyone other than my daughter. After a while my excitement got the best of me and I let a long-time friend of mine, Betty Allstot read it. She liked it and agreed that I should try to get it published. That was not enough for me. I had put so much of myself into this book that if it got rejected, I didn't know if I could handle it.

Soon I let yet another good friend, Kay McGraw read it. She loved the story and insisted I follow through and share Santa's First Gift with the world. So I did.

I found my illustrator, MaryJoyce Keary. I found Jesse Diamond to help with PR. And, I found Megan McGrew, my Graphic Artist. In just a few short months, we did it. We got the story ready to publish.

Thank you to all of these people and others who have inspired and supported me through this endeavor.

Humble Beginnings

Nick and Rebekah, or Reb as Nick liked to call her, lived in Bethlehem a long time ago. Nick worked at the stables belonging to a local inn. Most of the travelers and wealthy citizens of Bethlehem kept their animals at this stable. Nick and Reb were very poor but that didn't stop them from being generous. When there was a sick animal, Nick would take it home and together they would nurse it back to health. When a child broke a toy, Nick would fix it. And when someone in town had a question that couldn't be answered, he would secretly go and ask Reb. She always knew what to say.

Reb was very wise. She was the eighth of twelve children. When she was growing up she didn't stay home with her mother to learn how to cook and run a home like the other girls. Instead she would go to work with her father, who was a gold smith, or with her grandfather, who was a farmer. Often times, you could find her outside the synagogue sitting in her special secret hiding place listening to the priests, lawmakers, and wise men of the town holding important discussions. During these discussions, they would make vital decisions that affected everyone in the town.

In Reb's time, women were not allowed to hold influential positions in the government or church. Girls did not even go to school. They were to stay home to learn to cook and clean for their families.

One day, while sitting outside the synagogue, Reb found a book. With that book, she taught herself to read and write. She also learned all about man's beginning; the creation, and how God will send a savior. She learned the ways of her people and their history. With Reb's unique outlook on life and all of this knowledge, Reb became very wise.

Nick was a good-hearted, honest stable hand who was quite poor. He and Reb had their own way of doing things, usually not according to the old traditions. Some of the town's people felt threatened by Nick's and Reb's non-traditional ways.

It was mainly two men who did not like or trust Nick and Reb; Mr. Hie and Mr. Mytee. Being two of the top lawmakers, they were threatened by Nick's honesty and generosity and especially by Reb's intelligence. Mr. Hie and Mr. Mytee would hold town meetings often. Most of these meetings would have little to do with town business. Their purpose was to spread rumors and lies about Nick and Reb, trying to get them banished from Bethlehem. On one occasion, Nick took a lamb home. It was not used as a sacrifice to God nor had it been a special Sabbath dinner. Instead, a couple of days later Nick returned the lamb to the stables. Mr. Hie and Mr. Mytee believed Nick and Reb had used this lamb for some form of sorcery.

At every town meeting it was another story like this, but most of the people of Bethlehem liked Nick and Reb. They would agree that it isn't normal to let an animal live in the house, but they could not believe that Nick and Reb were any kind of sorcerers. And certainly they could not banish Nick and Reb from their home.

"Rebekah, Reb! I'm home," Nick shouted happily as he walked through the door after a long day of work. Nick loved coming home to Reb. They had a small house without many furnishings but it was very warm and welcoming.

"Oh Hi, Nick." Reb gave Nick a hug and a kiss. "How was your day, my love?"

"Every day is wonderful because I get to come home to you," Nick replied.

"Be serious Nick," Reb said as she blushed rosily from her husband's kind words. Everyday Nick would surprise Reb with a different affectionate greeting.

"I am," Nick said sincerely.

"Yes, and I love you too, my dear," Reb replied sweetly. Then with a little puzzlement she asked, "Where is your staff?"

"I think I set it down somewhere," Nick answered smiling, sheepishly.

"Where?" Reb asked.

"Oh, I guess on the back of a supply cart of some travelers that are heading to the Sea of Galilee," Nick said as he made his way past Reb to the table.

"Oh Nick, that's the third staff you've lost since we've been married. And that hasn't even been quite a year yet. I say, you would lose your head if the good Lord hadn't attached it so well," Reb scolded.

"Yes. Could you imagine the look on a traveler's face if he were to find my head on his supply cart?" Nick said teasingly.

Nick and Rebecca both laughed.

"Well Nick," Reb said. "I'm not sure how dinner will be tonight. My mother always told me that someday I would regret not having learned how to cook."

"If it's good enough to eat, then we shall eat it. If not, I will just give it to the animals like before," Nick replied.

"What if the animals won't even eat it?" Reb asked.

"Then I will go out after everyone has gone to sleep and bury it real deep in the ground, so deep that even the worms won't have to try it," Nick answered. They both laughed.

"Now go wash up and let's eat," Reb told Nick.

The dinner was indeed eaten all up. It wasn't very good but Nick was very hungry.

A Special Day

A few days later, Nick was at work cleaning the stables and feeding the animals. He would get some animals ready to leave with their caravan then clean the spaces for taking in new animals. As he worked he sang and danced. If he wasn't singing and dancing, he was talking to the animals.

On this particular day, Mr. Hie was outside the stables with his son Joseph.

Joseph was playing with his toy top. Joseph got excited and spun the top too hard. It hit a rock and broke the tip off. Joseph sadly picked it up and took it to his father.

"Father, can you fix my top, please?" Joseph asked.

Mr. Hie replied, "I don't have time to be bothered with your silly toy."

Joseph ran inside the stables crying.

"What's wrong?" Nick asked.

"I broke my top and my father won't fix it," Joseph answered.

"Well, let me take a look at that. All we need to do is file this down just a little bit…like this… and then….we'll take a very small sliver of wood and push it in this hole with the tip like this…. And huh…there you go, just as good as new." Nick gave it a spin.

It was as good as new, maybe even better.

"Oh thank you very much Mr. ah ah ah, Mr. Nick," Joseph said.

"Now you run along and have fun," Nick told him.

Joseph ran out of the stables yelling and whooping and hollering with joy.

Mr. Hie saw Joseph running and screaming and he didn't like it at all. He didn't like Nick taking time during his work day to fix a child's toy, especially his child's toy. So Mr. Hie walked into the stables only to see the leader of a large caravan giving Nick a one week old baby donkey. Mr. Hie overheard the traveler say...

"We can't take the poor little fellow with us. You know his mother isn't producing enough milk and he is much too young to travel. Besides, you have taken such good care of him already. I have seen you taking care of the all of the animals, you are good to them. I think he thinks you're his parent anyway. I know he will have a good home with you as his owner," the traveler said.

"I will have him strong and healthy when you return for him," Nick replied.

"I will not be returning. He is yours to keep," the traveler said.

Mr. Hie stepped in and said, "I will buy the little donkey from you sir. Here is a silver coin. That should more than cover the price of this weak and sickly creature."

"I'm sorry but this little donkey is no longer mine to sell. I have already given him to Nick. You will have to do your negotiating with him," the traveler replied.

Mr. Hie didn't want Nick to have the donkey, but even more, he didn't want to pay Nick a whole silver coin for this poor excuse for an animal. Mr. Hie turned to Nick and said, "I will give you two large chickens for that sickly donkey. Look at him, he is so weak that he can't even hold up his left ear. It is bent over."

"What is this?" the traveler asked. "When the donkey was thought to be mine you were willing to pay a whole silver coin for him. Now you only offer Nick two chickens."

"That's alright," Nick said to the traveler. Then Nick turned to Mr. Hie and said, "The donkey is not for sale. I have special plans for this little fellow."

Mr. Hie stormed off in anger.

"I'm glad you didn't sell the donkey to Mr. Hie. I didn't want him to have this little guy. Why are Mr. Hie and Mr. Mytee always so cruel to you?" the traveler asked.

Nick told the traveler a story of when he was younger. A prophet had come into town and said God had a wonderful plan for him. Mr. Hie and Mr. Mytee have been jealous of this and ever since have been looking for ways to make sure this wonderful plan doesn't come about.

Nick thanked the traveler and went on his way with the donkey following behind him.

Two weeks later the donkey had really grown and gotten a lot stronger. Other travelers had seen Nick and the donkey and had generously given Nick food for the donkey.

Now, the special day had come. The day Nick would take the donkey home.

At home, Reb had been trying to make a very special stew. The chickens she had were still too small to butcher so she settled on making a vegetable stew. She picked the biggest and best vegetables she could find for the stew. She even went out into the fields and picked some special secret herbs that her grandfather had shown her. After getting the stew started to cook, Reb got out the eight-foot stick of wood she had been working on for days. It was now taking good form and one could see that it will become a very large walking staff; when she cuts the large ball off the top. But Reb didn't. She took some dyes that she had made and painted the staff white. After that had dried, she painted a red swirl up the entire length and finished by painting the ball at the top red, too. Now it was ready. Reb was almost bursting with excitement as she hid the staff in the kitchen.

Soon Nick came whistling up to the front door. Reb's heart skipped a beat when Nick flung open the door and walked in. "Happy Anniversary!" they both shouted and then hugged and kissed each other.

"I will always and forever love you Reb," Nick said.

"And we will always and forever be together," Reb replied. "I have something for you Nick." Then Reb went and got the eight-foot staff and handed it to Nick. "It is large and brightly colored so you won't lose it."

"Thank you! This is great! It must have taken you days to make. How did you get such bright colors on it?" Nick asked.

"I still have a few secrets up my sleeves," Reb teased with a little wink.

"And now, I have a very special surprise for you. Close your eyes and come outside," Nick said as he led Reb by the hand and helped her out the door. Gently Nick turned Reb so she was face-to-face with the donkey colt. "Now open your eyes."

Reb opened her eyes. "Oh Nick, we can't afford a donkey. How much did he cost?" Reb asked.

"Not even as much as one straw from the broom you use to sweep up the dirt on the floor with," Nick told her.

"That's impossible." Reb thought out loud and then asked "You didn't steal him?"

"Nonsense!" Nick explained to Reb how the donkey was given to him and how for the last two weeks people had been giving food for the donkey to eat.

Reb understood and graciously accepted the gift by first giving Nick a big hug around his neck and then she hugged the donkey.

"What are you going to name him?" Nick asked.

Reb thought it about it for a while. "The color and feel of his fur reminds me of when I was a child. As the evenings turned cool, my grandmother would let me snuggle next to her and she would pull her old brown taffeta wrap around us. It made me feel warm and secure. In honor of my grandmother and her old brown taffeta wrap, I will call him Taffy," she answered.

"Taffy!" Nick repeated. "What kind of name is Taffy?"

"I think it is a sweet name," Reb answered.

"Well, he's your donkey. If you want to call him something silly like Taffy, then that is what we shall call him," Nick conceded.

"Let's go in and eat now," Reb said. "I worked all day on the stew. It should be good. I had almost forgot about the bread and just made it at the last minute so it might not be good or it may be under done."

Together they walked into the kitchen of their tiny house. Reb had set the table with some wild flowers she had picked, the only two matching bowls they had, two not-so-matching cups, and two spoons. While Nick washed up Reb got the pot of stew from the stove and put it on the table. She retrieved the bread from the oven and broke some pieces off.

"It smells wonderful dear," Nick said after washing up.

"Thank you, Nick," Reb said, blushing with pride. "I hope it tastes as good as it smells."

They sat down to the perfectly set table and looked at each other lovingly. Slowly Reb dished up the stew, first Nick's bowl and then hers. They each took a piece of the bread then Nick said the blessing. The smell of the stew made their mouths water as they eagerly dove their spoons into their bowls. Together they tasted it.

"Yuck!" Nick said as he spat out the stew. Reb had spit her stew out just as quickly. "This is awful!" Nick continued.

Reb lowered her head, and her eyes filled with tears. Just as she was about to start sobbing, Nick burst out laughing.

"What is so funny?" Reb asked crossly.

"Why this is the worst tasting stew ever made. I doubt anyone will ever make anything worse," Nick said through his laughter.

"What is so funny about that?" Reb asked as her frown deepened.

Nick answered, "What is so funny, is that the harder you try and the longer you work on a dinner, the worse it is and you know I'm not picky. I've always been impressed with you being you, my wife who can't cook. I love you just the way you are."

Reb realized he was right. It was funny that the longer and harder she tried to impress Nick with a good meal, the worse the meal turned out.

"The expression on your face when you tasted the stew…" Reb giggled. Then they both laughed.

"Well," said Reb, "we should be able to eat the bread. I just threw it together at the last minute so according to your theory it should be pretty good."

They laughed and ate the bread. It was indeed, good!

"Should I take the stew down to the stables and see if the animals will eat it or just wait until later and bury it after everyone in town has gone to bed?" Nick asked.

"Let's at least let the animals try it, but if they don't eat it, I don't want to know. Oh, and don't give any to Taffy. I don't want him to get the wrong idea about us. And don't let anyone see you," Reb answered.

A Special Night

Nick looked out the door. It was dark out now so he felt sure no one would see him. He picked up the pot of stew and went down to the stables. Nick poured a little of the stew on the donkeys' feed. At first they just sniffed at it with curiosity but eventually they tasted it. They stomped and brayed but went back for more. Nick put a little more on their food and they gobbled it down. He gave some to the camels and their reaction was the same. As Nick gave all the animals more, every drop was gobbled up. Anything that the stew even touched was eaten.

Nick dropped the pot, ran back to the house and got Reb.

"Quick! Quick! Reb, you've got to see this," Nick shouted.

"What is it?" Reb asked as she grabbed her shawl and ran out of the house.

"The animals love your stew!" Nick exclaimed as they reached the stable.

But when they looked into the stable their eyes got bigger than a harvest moon. "DUCK!" Nick shouted.

Reb ducked just in time as a donkey flew over her head.

"What is going on?" Reb asked in amazement.

"I don't know," Nick said. "There must have been something in your stew that makes the donkeys fly."

Then a camel flew by. "And camels too," Reb added. "Oh I do hope no one sees this! If anyone in town finds out what we did we will surely be banished from Bethlehem!"

"No one is going to see anything. At least all the animals are in the stable. Let's just calm them down and hope it wears off soon," Nick said.

Nick and Reb worked hard for over an hour calming all the animals. They were confident that all the animals were done flying. Nick started to open the doors to go home when suddenly a donkey came from behind them and flew right out the doors. Nick and Reb stared in wonder as the donkey zoomed up to the top of the roof of the stable.

The donkey stood on the roof while Nick tried to coax it down with some barley. But the donkey was too scared. Finally, Nick had to climb up to the donkey and gently lower him down with ropes, pulleys, and a harness. Reb thought everything was going to be fine but just before the donkey's hooves touched the ground, she saw Mr. Hie and Mr. Mytee lurking around the corner. "How long were they watching? How much had they seen?" she worried.

Nick practically flew off the roof himself to get to Reb as he saw the two men watching. Mr. Hie and Mr. Mytee looked at Nick and Reb, smiled an evil smile and then smugly turned and walked away. Reb looked at Nick hopelessly.

"Oh my dear sweet Reb, I am so sorry. I thought we had made it without anyone seeing anything. Now I will be the reason we will be banished from our own home. Can you ever forgive me?" Nick said.

"Nick," Reb replied. "I am the one to blame. If I had just stayed home as a little girl and learned how to cook this would not have happened! My cooking is the reason we will be banished from our home. Can you ever forgive me?"

"And on our anniversary, too," they both acknowledged.

Nick hugged Reb as she cried on his shoulder.

The Meetings

The very next day Mr. Hie and Mr. Mytee called an emergency town meeting. The sole purpose of this meeting was to accuse Nick and Reb of being sorcerers and banish them from Bethlehem, forever.

Everyone who could make it to the meeting, did. They wanted to show their support for Nick and Reb.

Mr. Mytee started the meeting. Everyone listened as Mr. Mytee told the tale of how he had seen Reb cook all day just to have Nick slip out after dark and feed it to the animals or sometimes, bury it.

"Surely this must be a form of sorcery." Mr. Hie suggested.

Everyone agreed that this was peculiar behavior but really none of their business.

Next, Mr. Hie told a story. "I was outside the stables where Nick works and my son Joseph was playing nearby. I had warned him before not to go into the stables when Nick was there. Suddenly my son started to cry. I tried to comfort him but couldn't. Then I saw Joseph go into the stable anyway. Two minutes later he came out running and screaming as if he had seen the devil himself. I knew I couldn't catch up with my son, with my bad knee and all. Then, I heard a noise, and when I looked over, I saw Nick standing in the stable door, laughing. To this day I don't know what really happened and my son hasn't offered to tell me. All I know is something or someone scared him, isn't that right Joseph?"

Mr. Hie turned to his son. Joseph tried to tell everyone that Nick actually just fixed his toy top and he was running and yelling for joy. Mr. Hie muffled Joseph's version of what happened and said "See, even now Joseph is so scared that he tries to make up stories to protect Nick."

The townspeople murmured amongst themselves.

Mr. Mytee quieted everyone down and then said "Let's not judge Nicolas and Rebekah until you hear everything."

Someone then yelled back, "You have asked us here every couple of months for a whole year now, trying to come up with some reason to banish Nick and Reb.

They have done nothing wrong. What do you and Mr. Hie have against them?" "You're just wasting our time," came another voice.

"Yes!" said yet another. "Once again the same stories. Next you will tell us again that Nick talks to the animals or that Reb sings at home while tending to her chores."

Yet another person added, "Or you'll tell that same old story of how Nick prays under the starry skies while walking in an open field when the law states that he is only supposed to pray in the synagogue. As we said before and will say again tonight, if you find this behavior so bad, then have one of our good priests talk with them, but let's not banish our neighbors and friends from their home."

Mr. Hie and Mr. Mytee just sat back with smiles on their faces. This just helped build their case against Nick and Reb and lead up to their next story.

Mr. Hie said, "People, people, I understand you have heard all these things before and you will stand by your neighbors. I respect you; I even appreciate you for your loyalty. But, I have a story that Nick and Reb cannot explain away and a high priest would not be able to council them on."

At this point some people started to leave the meeting saying "Not again. When will they ever quit?"

Mr. Hie shouted, "Wait friends, wait. You have not heard the worst of it. I have seen a donkey on the top of the stable where Nick works."

Everyone who had been leaving stopped and came back in to listen.

Mr. Hie continued, "Last night Mr. Mytee and I were out for a walk and heard quite a ruckus coming from the stable. As we walked closer, we saw that Nick and Reb were there doing something to the animals. Then, all of a sudden, a donkey came FLYING out the front doors of the stable and FLEW up to the roof top! I don't know how they could make a donkey fly, do you?"

"NO!!" shouted the people. "Donkeys can't fly. You must be mistaken. YOU are the ones who need help from a high priest."

"Tell them Nick," Mr. Mytee said. "Tell them what happened last night. How did that donkey get onto the roof?"

"NO!" the people shouted again.

One person said, "Tell us it is not true and we will believe you for we know you are honest people."

Nick got up to speak. Reb stood by his side and cried. "You all know me as an honest man. So I cannot deny what they say, for it is true."

"Tell the people how you made the donkey fly. You must have performed a sort of sorcery," urged Mr. Hie.

"No!" said Nick firmly. "You do what you must but I will not dishonor my wife and myself in front of all our friends."

Mr. Hie said, "We cannot have people like this living in our town. They can't be helped, they are sorcerers. They are an embarrassment and disgrace to our community and dangerous to have around, especially around our children. Remember the prophet saying our town is in store for great things. We have to keep it clean of all rubble. The only option we have is to banish them from Bethlehem, forever, before any more damage is done."

The crowd joined in, some reluctantly, but in the end they all agreed that Nick and Reb were no longer welcome to live in their town. Finally it was decided that Nick and Reb would be banished from Bethlehem and sent out to go as far north as they could go.

Of course everyone in the town knew that meant they would end up settling down somewhere north of the Sea of Galilee. But Nick and Reb saw things differently.

On The Move

Nick and Reb were given only one week to pack up all their belongings and say their good-byes to everyone.

Reb and her mother slowly packed up the household. "There's not much to pack," Reb told her mother. "It shouldn't take long."

When they finished packing the kitchen they went into the bedroom. There in the far corner of the room was a cradle.

"This cradle is very special, Mother," Reb said. "Nick made it and gave it to me as a wedding present. It will go on the top of the cart so it won't get broken."

Meanwhile, Nick had been to the stables. He was saying good-bye to all the animals. Taffy followed right behind Nick, for he didn't want to get left behind. Nick and Taffy slowly made their way back to the house.

Finally they had everything packed on the cart and ready to go. Taffy pulled the cart while Nick led the way. Reb and their dog followed behind with the sheep. The chickens rode on the cart with everything else.

Everyone they knew in Bethlehem, except for Mr. Hie and Mr. Mytee, walked them to the city limits and said their good-byes. Many tears fell as Nick and Reb turned to continue on the long journey ahead of them.

With Taffy's first step outside the city limits, the wheel of the cart went over a bump and caused the cradle to fall off. As if in slow motion, Nick and Reb watched as the cradle hit the ground and break into many pieces. They paused and stared at each other sadly for only a moment, then continued on their way.

The trip north was long and eventful. Nick, Reb, and Taffy met many interesting people and creatures. They saw many beautiful sights, too. Some of the people and other animals were mean and scary, but most were very friendly and helpful. Many a time a family would invite Nick and Reb to stay the night in their home and share their dinner with them. Sometimes different languages would slow the communication down but usually simple gestures for eating and sleeping were used and understood by all.

Taffy enjoyed the nights when Nick and Reb found a home and family that invited them to stay the night. He knew that would mean fresh hay for him to eat and a soft bed of straw to sleep on.

On nights they didn't have a home in which to sleep, they would just gather some wood for a fire and sleep under the open skies. This unwanted trip was having some positive effects on them. It was bringing them closer to each other and closer to God. It was teaching them how to survive and improvise in new and continually changing environments.

Days and weeks went on. They had long been out of Israel and through several other countries, too. Although the trip had been smooth for the most part, the continual travel had begun to take a toll on them. The sheep hardly wanted to move and the chickens were tired of riding on the cart for long hours. Taffy could barely pull the cart anymore. Reb was trying to keep her good cheer but even she was getting a little edgy now and then.

Finally, Nick stopped. All eyes turned to him, waiting for him to speak. As Nick turned and looked at everyone, he raised his staff high in the air and then stabbed it as hard as he could into the snow-covered ground. As he did, he declared, "I can travel no farther north."

"It is absolutely beautiful here," Reb told Nick. "But how will we make a house and a stable?"

"There were some trees a ways back," Nick replied. "I will set up a temporary shelter for us. We can settle in and rest up for a couple of days. Then Taffy and I will have to start making daily trips back and forth until we have enough logs to build our home and stable. I will build you the biggest house you have ever seen. We shall have the biggest house in all the North."

"Oh Nick, you always did promise to build me a large house someday. But, no matter the size, as long as I can share it with you, I will be happy," Reb replied.

Nick and Reb worked together to set up their tents. One was set up for them and one for the animals, but Taffy ended up sleeping in theirs. "To help keep us warm," Nick and Reb justified. After a couple of days, Nick and Taffy started their first trip back to where Nick had seen the trees. Reb packed them a lunch and sent them on their way early that morning.

What's Out There?

Soon after Nick and Taffy had disappeared from sight, Reb noticed something small moving around. Every time she tried to get a closer look it seemed to vanish into thin air. "My eyes must be playing tricks on me," Reb reasoned.

As evening drew near, Reb went outside once more. This time she saw Nick and Taffy returning. Taffy was pulling two logs behind him and they both looked exhausted. Reb ran out and helped Nick carry his tools back.

"You must be hungry and tired. Come in quickly and get something to eat. I will untie Taffy and get him fed," Reb said.

"Thank you, my love," Nick replied, using all the energy he had left to give Reb a smile.

Nick went in and ate while Reb untied the logs from Taffy. Reb could see that Taffy was hungry and tired as well. After the logs were untied she took him inside and got him some food. When Nick and Taffy were done eating, they both fell asleep.

The next morning Nick and Taffy got ready to go again. Reb packed them bigger lunches than the day before and reminded them to take a break or two so they wouldn't exhaust themselves.

When Nick went outside he said, "Why, thank you Reb! You knew just where I wanted the logs."

Reb looked out and said, "You're welcome, dear but that is not where I unloaded them last night."

Nick, Reb, and Taffy walked over to the logs and could see they had been moved from where Reb and Taffy had left them the night before. This was puzzling but Nick and Taffy had to get going. Nick kissed Reb and left with Taffy. Reb watched them until they were out of sight. She kept thinking she could see something following Nick and Taffy.

That day as Reb would work outside she felt a loneliness she hadn't felt the day before. This loneliness didn't scare her but it did seem to make the day longer.

Finally, Nick and Taffy returned. Once again Reb untied Taffy while Nick went inside to eat and rest. That evening Nick told Reb how he had cut many more trees but that Taffy could only tow back two each trip. Nick figured he and Taffy would be able to make three round trips a day, bringing two logs each trip. Reb decided she would make the trips with Taffy while Nick stayed in the woods and cut down more trees. The plans were agreed on before they slept that night.

The next morning they all ate a hardy breakfast. Reb grabbed the lunches that she had packed for them the night before. When they went outside, they saw a huge pile of logs.

"These are all the logs I cut down yesterday. How did they get here?" Nick wondered.

Reb thought this was a good time to tell Nick about what she thought she had seen a couple of days before and that perhaps her eyes were not playing tricks on her. Maybe they weren't as alone as they thought.

"It doesn't really make sense," Nick said. "Mysterious invisible creatures that don't communicate with us but are trying to help us?"

"We don't know who or what they are or why they are even helping us," Reb replied. "I think you and Taffy should go on as you have and I will watch for them here. Obviously they aren't trying to hurt us so I will be safe. Then tonight I will put some food out for them to thank them for their help."

That day, once again Nick cut down more trees than Taffy could bring back and once again that night the mysterious creatures brought back the ones that Taffy couldn't. Reb put out food for whomever was helping that evening and by morning it was all gone. This went on for days until one day Nick decided he had enough logs to make his big house for Reb.

Nick had designed the house in his head over and over again. He drew his plans out in the snow. It was late by the time he finished, but Nick wanted to put the first log in place before he went to bed that night. The next morning when Nick and Reb got up they looked outside and saw that these unseen creatures had changed Nick's plans. They had turned the house one quarter turn to the right and a couple of walls were almost completed.

That day Nick went on building the house according to the new plans. But, that night after everyone had gone to bed and were asleep, Reb got up and quietly slipped outside. There she saw polar bears, white snow bunnies, snow birds and reindeer all helping build the house. Reb was astonished. She didn't know if she should be afraid or happy. She did know she should be thankful. So Reb went back in and brought out some food to offer to the animals. At first the animals were afraid to get too close to Reb, but soon they realized that she meant no harm and started coming closer to her. Reb started to understand why she never could actually make out what these creatures were, as they were all white, just like the snow. Except for the reindeer, they must have just kept themselves hidden well, she thought.

Half the night Reb and the animals stayed up working together on the house. The next morning Reb told Nick what had happened. Nick found this hard to believe at first but he knew Reb wouldn't make something like that up, nor could she have done all that work by herself. That afternoon while Nick was working on the house, Reb went out and called for all the animals. One by one they came to her. When they were all there she called for Nick and Taffy to come and meet these animals. Nick thanked them for all their help and the improvements on the house plans. The animals seemed to know what he and Reb meant. Then they all went over to the house and worked together to build it big and strong.

In just a few short days the house was complete. It had a large kitchen, a yet-to-be-filled library, and an enormous living room with shutters that could be opened on the nicer days. There were so many bedrooms that Reb hadn't bothered to count them all. These were for all the children that Reb and Nick were planning to have.

Reb started moving in immediately. Nick then tried to explain to the animals that he would like to build a stable for his animals. He said that with their help he could build it big enough for all of them too. Nick drew out scaled down plans in the snow showing them all what the stable would look like and asked for suggestions for improvements. A polar bear came over and added a wing to the stable that Nick could use as a shop to build furniture and other things. The animals agreed to help build the new stable and shop. In just under two weeks, it too, was complete. All the animals had plenty of room and Nick had a place to make things.

Settling In

Nick and Reb were now settled in their new home and soon everyone got into their comfortable daily routine. Reb would cook and clean and visit with the animals while Nick would make furniture. He made more furniture than the house could hold.

A couple of years had passed. Nick and Reb loved their new home and new animal friends. Once in a while they would get a little homesick or want to talk to other people, but these feelings would pass and they were mostly happy. Reb and Nick still longed for children of their own but sadly none were to come.

Finally, Nick quit making furniture and started making statues out of the snow. He would pack the snow so hard it would turn to ice. Then he would carve a statue. The statues were short, like children, but had some characteristics of adults. But some features were different. They had pointy ears and shoes that curled up at the toe.

Reb would pretend sometimes that these statues were children. Seeing this, Nick made more. Soon he had made over a dozen statues. Nick would pick out names for each of them very carefully. They were Joseph, Peter, Mark, Paul, Luke, Daniel, Moses, Simeon, Jacob, Rachel, Martha, Mary, Ruth, and Leah. These were all names he had heard in church and from his family.

Reb and Nick put their hearts and souls into taking care of the statues. Sometimes Taffy would get a little jealous of the time they spent on the statues. Every morning Nick and Reb brushed away the new fallen snow and if the sun from the previous day had started to melt them, Nick would lovingly and patiently make the necessary repairs. Knowing that Taffy sometimes needed special attention, Reb would slip Taffy an extra treat or spend an entire day with him and then everything would be alright.

The Good News

One morning Nick and Reb awoke to the noise of the animals. When they looked out their door it appeared as if the animals were having a meeting. The birds were chirping when a bunny interrupted by stomping his foot on the snow several times. Then the bears all growled together while the reindeer put one front leg back and lowered their heads like they were bowing in agreement. After they had all agreed they started towards the house chirping, growling, stomping and dancing around.

Nick and Reb walked out to meet them. Once again the animals all started their chirping, growling, stomping and dancing around as if to tell Nick and Reb something. Even Taffy was braying to Nick and Reb. Nick and Reb felt bad that they could not understand.

"Is there a storm coming?" Nick asked.

The deer shook their heads to say no.

"Are there more people coming?" Reb asked.

The bears growled and shook their furry heads.

"What is going on?" they asked

Then the birds started chirping frantically amongst themselves and flew away.

"Oh, no," said Reb. "We've made them mad at us, Nick."

"I don't think so, dear. See the rest of the animals are staying," Nick replied.

Everyone went on about their daily routines. Nick took care of the statues while Reb cooked and cleaned. Reb never spent much time on cooking and the meals were getting pretty good. Nick dusted the snow off of the statues and had some repairs to do from the previous day's warm sun. Taffy and the deer got more logs from the woods to burn for heat. The bunnies gathered food for the chickens and the polar bears kept watch over the sheep. They knew they were not allowed to eat the sheep, but it didn't take much work and they could usually take a long afternoon nap.

Around midafternoon the birds returned. One had something in its beak. He landed at Nick's feet and dropped it. Nick picked it up. It was a headline from a newspaper. The birds had flown all the way to the nearest town to pick up the newspaper article but only the headline was left when they got back to the North Pole. Reb came running over.

"What does it say?" she asked.

Nick read the headline out loud.

It read, "THE MESSIAH TO BE BORN ON DECEMBER 25TH OF THIS YEAR! YOUR GIFTS ARE WELCOME"

"Oh Nick, we must take a gift to the Messiah," Reb said.

"Yes," Nick answered, "but what? There is nothing here worth anything."

"Bite your tongue, Nick," Reb said. "You are very good with your hands and wood. You could make something. I know! You could make a bed for him." She had wanted to say cradle but just couldn't since hers had broken the first day of their trip.

"I don't think the Messiah will need a bed," Nick said. "He will have everything."

"Well, you're probably right," Reb replied. Then after a pause she added, "But what about a toy? All children like toys and the Messiah will be a child at first. You used to fix children's toys all the time. I bet you could make the best toy in the world."

Nick thought about it and said, "You're right, Reb. We shall give the best gift of all to the Messiah."

The next day Nick started on the toy. He chopped a chunk of wood off of one the logs that Taffy and the deer had brought back. At lunch time Reb came out to the shop and asked Nick what he was doing.

"I'm working on the Messiah's gift, of course," Nick answered.

"You're silly, that's not for another four months," Reb said.

"I know, but I'm excited about it now so I thought I would get started," Nick said.

"What are you going to do when you are finished with that toy and you are still excited?" Reb asked.

"Maybe I'll make two or three toys and give him the best one," Nick said. "Hey dear, where did the newspaper say the Messiah would be born?"

"Oh my, …I, …I don't think it said," Reb said as she retrieved the clipping from her pocket. "It just says 'THE MESSIAH TO BE BORN ON DECEMBER 25TH OF THIS YEAR! YOUR GIFTS ARE WELCOME'."

"Where should we take the toy then, Reb?" Nick asked.

"I don't know, but I know we have to make sure the Messiah gets our gift," Reb replied.

Nick and Reb looked at each other puzzled as to what to do.

Finally Reb broke the silence and said, "I have an idea but it will take a lot of work."

"What is it?" Nick asked hurriedly.

"You could make a toy for every child in the world. Then we would know that the Christ child has received our gift," Reb said.

"Yes, that would take a lot of work but as long as Taffy and the deer don't mind making more trips to get more wood, I'm sure I can make the toys," Nick said.

"I know you can do it, Nick," Reb replied and then added, "If only our snow statues were real, then they could help us make the toys for all the children."

"I have one more question, Reb. How will we deliver toys to all the children around the world? It took us a long time to get here. It would take even longer to travel with a bunch of toys stopping at every house to give one to every girl and boy," Nick wondered out loud.

"You're right, but we have to do it somehow. You just work on the toys and I will work on a way for us to deliver them," Reb said.

The Plan

Nick set to working on making the toys while Reb went in the house thinking. In just an hour Nick came in. His first toy was done and he was very proud when he handed it to Reb to show her his craftsmanship.

It was a stick puppet and Reb thought it was adorable even though she could see where Nick had cut it a little too deep in a couple of places and it was still a little too rough for a baby's toy. She said, "You did a great job. Any child would be glad to receive such a fine toy."

"Have you thought of a way we can deliver all the toys?" Nick asked.

"I think I have," Reb answered. "Remember our first anniversary?"

"Yes," Nick said cautiously. "I thought we were trying to forget that tragic day."

"That tragedy may end up being a blessing," Reb said.

"What do you mean?" Nick asked.

Reb answered, "You and I believe everything happens for a reason, everything has a purpose, right?"

Nick nodded in agreement.

Reb continued, "Then maybe the purpose of that meal was to help us now. What I mean is, the dinner that we thought was a disgrace may have actually been God's Grace. Don't you see, if I can recreate that stew, we could feed it to Taffy."

Nick interrupted Reb and said, "You didn't want Taffy to have any of the stew last time."

"Hear me out," Reb said. "If we feed it to Taffy and we put all the toys in our cart and harness Taffy to the cart, then Taffy can fly us around the whole world. You and I can deliver all the toys to all the good little girls and boys. And, since there are children in Bethlehem, we will have to go there as well and get to see our old home."

"Reb, you are a genius," Nick said. "I knew you could think of a way! You are so smart."

"We should go to Bethlehem last," Reb said.

"I don't want our gift to the Christ Child to be late so I think we should head out on the night of the 24th," Nick said.

"Great idea," Reb said. "It should be late enough by the time we get to Bethlehem that no one will see us."

"I want to check on the animals at the stable where I used to work," Nick added.

"Of course, we will do that; it can be the very last thing we do," Reb said.

"I sure hope Taffy's not afraid of flying," Nick said joyfully.

They both laughed until Reb realized she might be the one afraid of flying!

As the weeks passed everyone was busy helping get ready for the big trip. Taffy and the deer brought many logs back for Nick. Nick continued to make more toys. The bunnies and bears designed a new cart for Nick and Reb. It was much larger and more comfortable than their cart was and it was designed to fly better. It didn't have wheels but skids instead. This was to help make the take-offs and landings smoother for Taffy.

Reb had been trying to recreate their anniversary dinner, the one that got them banished from their home. The problem was that she had become a pretty good cook now, so it was quite hard for her to make a meal that no one could eat. Then she remembered what Nick said that night of their anniversary. "The longer and harder you work on a meal, the worse it turns out."

"That's it!" she said to no one but herself. "I've become a pretty good cook because I don't spend much time on meals anymore. Just like now, I am in a hurry to recreate that stew. I need to recreate the whole process."

Reb sat down and made a list of all the ingredients that she had used before. The list included the biggest and best vegetables and the special herbs that her grandfather had shown her. But Reb didn't have a garden any more, nor were there fields to find the herbs. She decided that she would just have to go to town. She would take some of the extra furniture that Nick had made to trade for these ingredients.

Reb told Nick her plans to go to town to get everything. Nick told her that he couldn't finish all the toys and the new sleigh before the 24th if he went with her. Reb said that would be fine. She would take Taffy with her and the birds could lead the way. Everything was set and Reb left early the next morning.

While Reb was gone, Nick looked over all the toys he had made. There were tops, little dolls, carved animals, toy carts, and more stick puppets. By now Nick had gotten pretty good at making toys, and even he could see that his first stick puppet wasn't all that good. He decided that it wasn't good enough to give to a child and he would just put it in the burn pile.

When Reb and Taffy returned late the next day Reb was excited. She had found all the ingredients she needed to make her stew. She couldn't wait to get started the next morning.

As with the last time, Reb got up early in the morning and carefully repeated every step of the recipe. When Nick came in that night for dinner Reb had him taste the stew and just like before, Nick couldn't spit it out fast enough.

"THAT'S IT!!!" Nick exclaimed.

"We need to test it on one of the animals to be sure," Reb said.

"I will give a little bit of it to two of the reindeer, but if it is like before, it will only last a couple of hours," Nick said. "You will have to pack a lot of it with us on our trip so we can keep giving it to Taffy."

Nick and Reb took the stew outside to the reindeer. They tried to explain to the reindeer what might happen but the deer didn't seem to understand. The reindeer ate the stew and in no time they were flying all over. Nick turned to Reb, grabbed her and gave her a big hug. "You did it! You're the greatest!"

The Trip

The next morning was December 24th and the reindeer were still flying around.

Reb and Nick noticed this and hoped the stew would keep Taffy flying all night.

Reb asked Nick, "Are you ready to go out tonight, dear? It will be the greatest adventure we've ever been on. Maybe even greater than any adventure anyone has ever been on."

"Yes," Nick answered. "All the toys are made, the sleigh is built and loaded, all we have to do is to wait for evening. Then we can feed Taffy the stew and away we will go."

"We won't be going until later so we should make sure all our statues are fine and that the other animals will be all right while we are gone," Reb said.

Nick agreed and the two headed over to the statues.

Meanwhile, Taffy and the birds had been playing together. The birds were trying to show Taffy how to take off, fly, and land. But of course Taffy couldn't really do any of these until he had eaten the stew. So, Taffy would jump up as high as he could, then run for a ways and then stop as if he were taking off, flying and landing. This went on for a while and Taffy was getting pretty good at it. Forgetting to be careful though, Taffy jumped too high. When he came down his hoof landed on a piece of wood. Taffy fell and couldn't get back up. The birds rushed over to get Nick and Reb. When they got back, Taffy had big tears in his eyes. He couldn't move it hurt so bad.

The two flying reindeer flew to the stable and came back with the cart. Nick loaded Taffy in it and they all took Taffy back to the stable.

Reb gently wrapped Taffy's front right leg and informed everyone that it was broken. "We won't be able to go tonight," she announced. "Taffy can barely walk with a broken leg, but there is no way he could fly and land with it."

"We will just have to wait until his leg heals then," Nick said.

Everyone was quiet. No one knew what to do but everyone knew they had to deliver the toys that night.

It was Reb who finally broke the silence. "No!" she said. "The toys have to be delivered tonight to make sure the Messiah gets our gift. I have been terrified of the idea of flying ever since we started this plan. I will stay here with Taffy. Nick, you will have to go without me."

"But who will pull the sleigh?" Nick asked. "You so wanted to see Bethlehem. And you were going to make sure we kept flying by feeding the stew to Taffy when we made our stops."

Just then the two reindeer who had tested the stew earlier flew overhead and landed next to Nick, as if to volunteer for the job.

"That's it!" Nick exclaimed. "One of the deer can fly and pull the sleigh for me. We will only need to feed him the stew once before I go since it lasts so much longer on the reindeer."

"That's a great idea," Reb said. But knowing she needed to make Taffy feel better she added, "But you had better take two reindeer. The sleigh is very heavy and they aren't as strong as Taffy."

All the animals were in a flutter, even Taffy was excited to know the trip would not be cancelled.

While Nick took care of hitching the reindeer to the sleigh, Reb saw the first little stick puppet sitting on the burn pile. She thought Nick had accidently dropped it there so she picked it up and tossed it onto the sleigh. It fell to the bottom.

Soon the deer were hitched to the sleigh full of toys with Nick at the reins. It was evening now, time to leave.

"Good luck my dear," Reb shouted to Nick. "I love you always. And if you see the Christ child, thank him."

"I will my darling," Nick shouted back. "And I love you too, always and forever, together."

Then Nick turned to the reindeer and gave the command, "Up, up and away!"

Soon Nick and the deer came to their first stop. The landing was smooth. Nick said to the deer, "You can see from the number of shoes outside the door that this family has four children. I'll just take four gifts in with me." Nick quietly opened the door and slipped the four toys in the house without waking a soul.

"This is pretty easy," Nick told the deer. "Let's go on to the next house. Up, up and away!" He was starting to like saying that.

The deer flew to the next house. Nick pointed out to the deer that seven children live here and so he took seven gifts in with him. Once again he slipped in and out without waking anyone.

Soon the deer were counting the shoes and giving Nick the gifts to take in and leave for the children. Each stop seemed to take less time than the one before. Town to town they went, giving all the children a gift. Finally, they stopped in Bethlehem.

The Gift

"Oh, no, not here, not yet," Nick said to the reindeer. "Bethlehem is our last town."

But the reindeer just counted out the gifts for Nick. Then Nick understood that they were at their last town as there were only enough toys left in the sleigh for the children of Bethlehem. They had visited all the other homes all around the world. Nick gave all the children in Bethlehem and around the world a toy and he then realized he had not even seen the Christ child. After he had pondered for a bit, Nick concluded that he must have given the Christ child a toy but he just hadn't recognized Him. Satisfied with his conclusion, Nick decided to look in on the animals in the stable where he used to work.

As he got closer to the stable, he saw more animals than usual. There were so many sheep, camels, and donkeys. All the animals were circled around something. Then Nick noticed people were there, too. There were three wise men, a lot of shepherds, and even a little shepherd boy playing a drum. He saw many others were carrying gifts. Nick wondered what was going on. Just then Nick saw the faces of Mary and Joseph as Mary laid down a baby in a manger. "THAT IS the Christ Child," Nick trembled joyfully.

Nick went back to the sleigh to get a gift for the baby and saw only one small toy lying on the bottom of the sleigh. It was the very first toy he had made. But how had it gotten in the sleigh? He had put it in the burn pile.

"This is not good enough for the Christ Child," Nick told the deer. "What should I do? What would Reb want me to do? I know, I will just tell the baby that I have run out of gifts and that I will return with a toy for him on his first birthday."

Nick started towards the Christ child but the two reindeer stopped him just as Mary and Joseph looked up and saw him. One of the deer nudged him with the small, less than perfect toy. Nick held the toy and looked at it. He realized the imperfections holding him back were not in the toy but in his pride. This was the very first toy Nick had made and this one was the one that Nick had put more of his heart into than all the other toys.

Nick took the toy and walked over to the manger. He saw the most beautiful, loving, forgiving face ever. Nick knew the baby would understand and know that this gift came from Nick's and Reb's own hearts.

He thought that everyone was watching to see what gift he would give the Messiah as he walked up to add it to the pile. How embarrassed Nick was to have to put this small toy down amongst all the other bigger and more prestigious gifts. Nick smiled at Mary and Joseph and walked around to the other side of the manger. He was hoping that no one would notice the gift. Only the Christ child watched Nick as he went around the manger, but Nick was unaware of this.

He looked for a place to hide his gift and finally found one. Slowly he released the precious toy into the Baby's other gifts. As the toy left his hands and became the Baby's possession an angelic glow began to form around it. Nick was startled. He looked at the baby and saw Jesus smile at him. Suddenly, Nick was pleased and at peace with this gift. Nick was filled with the truest spirit of CHRISTmas.

When Nick got home he was still overjoyed with the gift he had gotten from heaven. But heaven had given him more than he knew. Taffy was up running around and kicking, for his broken leg had healed. Reb was overwhelmed with excitement and peace at the same time. The statues' icy shells had been melted and their souls, made with God's love and from Nick's and Reb's hands were released from captivity. They had turned into what we now call elves. All of this had happened in that small instant when Nick gave Christ his heart.

It didn't take long for everyone, Nic, Reb, the elves, Taffy, the reindeer, bears, bunnies, and birds to recognize that this was their destiny. Every year they would make toys for all the children all over the world and every year Nick and the reindeer would deliver them on the night of December 24th.

To this day, Nick and Reb keep with the tradition. But no gift has ever been greater than the gift that was given that first Christmas.

The End

Made in the USA
San Bernardino, CA
16 October 2016